Men-at-Arms • 505

Imperial Chinese Armies 1840–1911

Philip S. Jowett • Illustrated by Gerry Embleton
Series editor Martin Windrow

First published in Great Britain in 2016 by Osprey Publishing
PO Box 883, Oxford, OX1 9PL, UK
PO Box 3985, New York, NY 10185–3985, USA
E-mail: info@ospreypublishing.com

Osprey Publishing, part of Bloomsbury Publishing Plc

A CIP catalogue record for this book is available from the British Library

Print ISBN: 978 1 4728 1427 2
PDF ebook ISBN: 978 1 4728 1428 9
ePub ebook ISBN: 978 1 4728 1429 6

Editor: Martin Windrow
Index by Alan Rutter
Typeset in Helvetica Neue and ITC New Baskerville
Originated by PDQ Media, Bungay, UK
Printed in China through Worldprint Ltd

16 17 18 19 20   10 9 8 7 6 5 4 3 2 1

Osprey Publishing supports the Woodland Trust, the UK's leading woodland
conservation charity. Between 2014 and 2018 our donations will be spent on
their Centenary Woods project in the UK.

www.ospreypublishing.com

Dedication

Philip Jowett would like to dedicate this book to his family.

Acknowledgements

Philip Jowett would like to thank Col Leslie Addington for permission to use an
image, and Prof Robert Bickers and Jamie Carstairs of the Chinese Historical
Photographs Project for their assistance. He also records his gratitude to John
Cloake for his help with researching this book and for his kind permission to
use photographs from his collection.

Artist's Note

Readers may care to note that the original paintings from which the colour
plates in this book were prepared are available for private sale. All reproduction
copyright whatsoever is retained by the Publishers. All enquiries should be
addressed to:

www.gerryembleton.com

The Publishers regret that they can enter into no correspondence upon this
matter.

IMPERIAL CHINESE ARMIES 1840–1911

INTRODUCTION

An eyewitness to the fighting around the Taku Forts in 1860 painted this cavalry sentry, wearing one of the wide variety of winter coats worn by Imperial troops. Most fur or fleece coats like this one were worn by soldiers from northern China and Manchuria, and wearing them in the southern provinces was regarded as effeminate. In the original painting the trooper's Manchu hat has a black brim and a red crown with a gold ornament or 'pommel' at the apex.

By 1840 the once-dynamic Qing (Ch'ing) Dynasty that had ruled the Chinese Empire since 1644 was in terminal decline. The Imperial government had allowed the administration of its vast territories to become passive, parochial and deeply corrupt. The Manchu regime, which was perceived by many of its Han Chinese subjects as essentially foreign, had overtaxed its peoples, discriminated against ethnic and religious minorities, and failed to meet the needs of a hugely increased population (from perhaps 125 million in 1736 to some 432 million by 1852). Consequently it was challenged by repeated regional rebellions, which became chronic during the mid-19th century.

Administrative weakness was mirrored in the steady decline of the once-proud Imperial army and navy, which had suffered humiliating setbacks during the 18th century. These included the defeat of three invasions of Burma in 1766–69, and a failed invasion of Vietnam in 1788. In 1794 the so-called White Lotus Rebellion, in protest against taxation, broke out astride the borders of Szechwan, Shensi and Hupeh provinces, and continued until 1804. While this and subsequent rebellions were eventually crushed, putting them down typically took many years, was ruinously destructive, and – since their suppression was achieved by provincial governors with locally raised forces – further weakened the Dynasty's central authority.

The constant threat of rebellions was compounded from 1839 by the intrusion of European military forces into Chinese territory from the port cities where Western traders had established themselves. A weakened China became the target for aggressive commercial policies pursued by European nations and the USA, and territorial expansion by Imperial Russia and Japan. Western demands for trade access to the interior were backed by full-scale military action by the British and French, both in eastern China and in Chinese vassal territories. The Dynasty's failure to offer effective resistance further weakened its prestige, thus sparking yet more rebellions.

The Qing Dynasty continued to resist both internal unrest and external aggression throughout the period covered by this book, but decades of constant political, military and financial pressure inevitably took their toll on the Imperial armies. By the time of the final Revolution in 1911 the fall of the Dynasty was unavoidable.

ANTI-DYNASTY REBELLIONS

In the mid-19th century the Dynasty was almost brought to its knees by a series of uprisings collectively known to history as the Taiping Rebellion. Covering an enormous area, these lasted from 1851 until 1866. By the time they guttered out they had caused some 20 million deaths, mostly amongst civilians, and major displacements of population. Huge armies were raised on both sides, and during those 15 years fighting raged over eight provinces. (For much fuller details, readers are recommended to Men-at-Arms 275, *The Taiping Rebellion*.)

The first phase of this cataclysm was the so-called Triad Revolt, which devastated Kwangsi and Kwangtung provinces in the south-east between October 1850 and March 1853. (When the rebels were defeated 100,000 of those who had been captured were beheaded, at a rate of some 8,000 per day.) Meanwhile, however, rebellion had spread northwards to the Yangtze river valley, and in the years that followed various Taiping armies – sometimes allied, sometimes in rivalry – would pursue major campaigns of manoeuvre that brought see-sawing victories and defeats. From their capital at Nanking, occupied from March 1853 until July 1864, the Taipings would dominate a vast area of eastern and central China, and against this backdrop more local uprisings broke out. Some of their leaders were inspired by and in contact with the Taiping movement, but other conflicts were specifically local, often sparked by religious or inter-ethnic hatreds.

From 1853 to 1855 the Small Sword Society Uprising took place in the region around the port of Shanghai in Kiangsu province; this was eventually put down by a joint Qing-French force, with the European power acting to protect its interests in this strategic trading centre (as it would during two future attempts on Shanghai, by Taiping forces). As this rebellion ended another broke out far to the south-west in Yunnan province; this Moslem-led Panthay Revolt lasted until 1873, and resulted in a million deaths – as in other such cases, the defeated rebel leaders

In photos from the 1890s it is hard to distinguish between military and civil officials by their dress. This young Imperial mandarin poses with men of his bodyguard, whose dual role was to protect the official and to act as public executioners of both civilian and military malefactors, such as bandits and rebels. In times of war 'police' and other Qing officials could be drafted into the army and sent to fight, with little or no military training. However, these men would probably have had plenty of practice in the use of their long, heavy swords.

MONGOLIA

Xinjiang

MANCHURIA

Harbin

Sungari River

Inner Mongolia

Jehol

Mukden

Kalgan

Fengtien

Peking

Tientsin

Chihli

Taiyuan

Shansi

Yellow River

Tsingtao

Kansu

Shantung

YELLOW
SEA

Shensi

Honan

Kiangsu

Szechwan

Hupeh

Anhwei

Nanking

Hankow

Shanghai

Yangtze River

Wuchang

Hangchow

Nanchang

Chekiang

EAST
CHINA
SEA

Kweichow

Hunan

Kiangsi

Yunnan

Fukien

Foochow

Kwangsi

Kwangtung

FORMOSA

Canton

VIETNAM

Hong Kong

KOREA

JAPAN

SEA
OF
JAPAN

SOUTH
CHINA
SEA

N

| 0 | | 250 miles |
| 0 | | 500 km |

and their families were cruelly executed, but the majority of the deaths were due to famine and disease. Other uprisings included the Red Turban Revolt (1854–56) in Kwangtung, and the Nien-Fei Rebellion (1853–68) which ravaged Honan and Anhwei provinces. Two Dungan Rebellions broke out in the largely Moslem Kansu province in the far north-west (in 1862–77, and 1895–96), and the religious element again added an extra savagery to these outbreaks and their suppression. Some local uprisings were triggered by heavy-handed Qing rule over various ethnic groups; for instance, during 1854–73 the Miao people of Kweichow province in the south-west rebelled for the third time in a century. Although such revolts were not, like the Taiping Rebellion, a direct challenge to Qing power, they inevitably put an additional strain on the resources and morale of the Imperial armies.

The Boxer Rebellion of 1900–01 began as an anti-Qing revolt but evolved into a campaign against the foreign intruders, which was subsequently aided by Imperial troops sent against the foreign legations in Peking by the Dowager Empress Tzu Hsi. While this fighting was going on in northern China, in the south the revolutionary leader Sun Yat-sen – whose Kuomintang party had long advocated the overthrow of the Dynasty – launched his Huizhou Uprising in October 1900. Although he raised 20,000 men and received Japanese aid, his uprising failed to attract much popular support. From exile in Japan he continued to plot against the Dynasty, which had been utterly humiliated by the international military occupation of Peking and its surrounding territory. After the death of the Dowager Empress in 1908, and her succession by the boy-emperor Pu Yi, the Dynasty's days were clearly numbered. The final anti-Qing rebellion was the Wuchang Uprising of October–December 1911, which became the Revolution that overthrew the 268-year old dynasty. In January 1912 the Chinese Republic was proclaimed under the presidency of Dr Sun Yat-sen (who within a matter of weeks would be replaced by a military warlord).

CONFLICTS WITH EXTERNAL ENEMIES

First Opium War, 1839–42 This war between British and Chinese forces broke out after Qing officials in the southern port of Canton ordered the seizure and destruction of imported opium in British warehouses and ships on 30 March 1839. The government was reacting to the creation of thousands of Chinese opium addicts to feed the trade in the drug, which was grown in large quantities in British-controlled India. In June a 5,000-strong British expeditionary force landed near Canton and advanced northwards against limited Chinese resistance. After a series of negotiations, a peace agreement, and the resumption of fighting in 1841, hostilities were finally ended by the Treaty of Nanking in August 1842. During the war the British had captured four other Chinese ports, and threatened the city of Nanking inland from Shanghai.

Sino-Sikh (or Dogra) War, 1841–42 In May 1841 the Sikh general Zorawar Singh, with Dogra vassal troops, invaded Qing-ruled western Tibet. Initially successful, they suffered badly in the Himalayan winter, and Zorawar was defeated and killed at Toyo on 12 December. A Qing/Tibetan advance into Ladakh the following spring was halted, and stalemate led to a peace treaty in August 1842.

Russian incursions into Manchuria, c.1849–60 In 1851 the Treaty of Kulja temporarily stabilized relations between Russia and China in the border country of western Xinjiang province. In 1854–57 a series of incursions by Russian-led Transbaikal Cossacks and settlers from Siberia into north-eastern Manchuria, by sailing down the Amur river, went largely unchallenged.

Second Opium ('Arrow') War, 1856–59 The excuse for this was the alleged failure of the Qing government to abide by the terms of the 1842 Treaty of Nanking

An illustration from an English newspaper of 1842 shows what most Europeans would have regarded as typical Chinese soldiers; accurate features are the smock with an identification disc, the officer's Manchu hat with trailing feather, the scalloped-edge flag, and the straight sword. At this date most soldiers were armed with swords, spears or other polearms, and bows; few Western firearms had reached the Imperial Army, and their matchlock muskets were archaic.

and other agreements that allowed Europeans to trade in China. Hostilities broke out in October 1856 after a British-registered opium ship, the *Arrow*, was seized. The war was initially fought in southern China; the British attacked forts protecting the port of Canton, and the city itself was briefly captured by Royal Marines before they were ordered to withdraw.

A few months of 'phoney war' followed; in 1857 the Indian Mutiny was making major demands on British manpower, and there was little support in Britain for a full-scale Chinese war. Using the mistreatment of missionaries as an excuse, the French joined a British plan to force China to negotiate, and in December 1857 Canton was retaken after an Allied bombardment. In April 1858 a naval force sailed northwards, and after a brief fight captured the Taku Forts, which protected the mouth of the Peiho river giving access to Tientsin south of Peking. This forced the Chinese to make further concessions to the Europeans and Americans by the Treaty of Tientsin (26 June). A year later a British squadron carrying diplomats sent to conclude the treaty was confronted by a 50,000-strong Chinese force in and around the reoccupied Taku Forts, commanded by the Mongolian general Sengge Rinchen. An assault on 25 June 1859 by a British landing force was driven off with 453 casualties, and after four British ships were lost the squadron withdrew.

This lithograph from a European magazine imagines an attack by Black Flag mercenaries against a French post during the Tonkin war of 1884–85; it shows small bamboo sun hats, long plain cotton tunics, and the broad trousers worn in the southern regions (see also Plate C3). Although the Black Flags fought alongside Imperial troops in Tonkin, it was a strictly pragmatic alliance: the Black Flags were essentially bandits, but were useful enough for the Imperial governors of frontier provinces to arm them against the foreign invaders of North Vietnam, and to give their leader Liu Yung-fu the local rank of general.

Third China War, 1860 This was simply a resumption of the Second Opium War after a pause to regroup. In May 1860 an expeditionary force was formed at Hong Kong with 11,000 British and 7,000 French troops, and on 2 August it successfully assaulted the Taku Forts. The Chinese defenders withdrew to Peking, followed by the Allies, and in September Chinese requests for a parley were followed by the arrest and cruel mistreatment of an Allied delegation. Although the Qing capital was in theory defended by some 20,000 troops plus a mobile cavalry force of 30,000, after the Allies arrived on 26 September the city fell with hardly a fight; the emperor fled, and on 6 October the Imperial Summer Palace was ransacked. Under the subsequent Treaty of Peking (18 October) China paid a huge indemnity, and made major territorial and trade concessions; an Allied garrison would remain in Tientsin. In November a forced Russo-Chinese treaty ceded all Manchurian territory north of the Amur river and east of the Ussuri – some 350,000 square miles – to Russia.

Sino-Russian clash, 1878 This brief conflict was fought in western Xinjiang province; superior Qing forces under the general Tso Tsung-t'ang checked an advance by poorly armed Russian settler militia.

Franco-Chinese War, 1884–85

Simultaneously with the Third China War (see above), the French Navy had annexed the southern half of the kingdom of Vietnam (then called Annam), a tributary state of the Qing Empire. Naval expeditions up the Mekong river captured and held Saigon in 1859–61; in June 1862 King Tu Duc of Annam ceded three of his southern provinces, and in 1867 the French annexed the rest of what they called Cochinchina.

North-east Tonkin, 1890: seated surrounded by his men is a leader named *Doi* Van – 'Sergeant Van', a deserter from the French-raised *Tirailleurs Tonkinois*, whose band regularly came down from the hills of the northern Yen The region to raid pacified areas. After the Franco-Chinese peace treaty of 1885 the frontier remained turbulent for at least 15 years; bandits maintained relationships of mutual profit with the Imperial mandarins on the Kwangsi frontier. The authorities allowed them to pass unhindered to sell their booty and slaves and to buy arms and ammunition, and it was not unknown for Kwangsi troops to mount cross-border raids of their own. Note that the members of this group carry modern bolt-action rifles; in the 1890s Winchester lever-action repeater rifles were also common. The umbrella is of a shape also used for straw hats in Tonkin.

Continued French pressure for trade access to the delta of the Red river in North Vietnam (Tonkin), and thence into Yunnan province, led to the seizure of Hanoi in April 1882 and subsequent expansion over the surrounding delta. A French defeat in May 1883 at the hands of the Black Flags (Chinese mercenaries-cum-bandits, who had spilled over the border after the Taiping Rebellion), was followed by the natural death of King Tu Duc. France then landed 5,000 troops around the Annamese capital, Hue, and in August declared a French protectorate over the whole of Vietnam, though it would take an expeditionary force enlarged to 15,000 to pacify the Red river delta. They were opposed by the Black Flags cooperating with local mandarins, and by Imperial troops from Yunnan and Kwangsi; the delta cities were cleared by spring 1884, but Kwangsi troops continued to resist up-country during the autumn. In August a naval and land war broke out between France and China (to the annoyance of the other powers, whose trade it disrupted). The French blockaded and shelled coastal cities, and in October made an ill-judged landing on Formosa. In Vietnam, French troops fought their way north in February 1885 and occupied the frontier town of Lang Son, but after a defeat just inside Chinese territory on 24 March they withdrew to the delta. In April 1885 a ceasefire was concluded, and another Treaty of Tientsin was ratified on 11 June; Chinese troops were officially withdrawn from Tonkin, but Chinese bandits remained, and its pacification would take 20,000 French troops about another 15 years.

Sino-Japanese War, 1894–95 Another Chinese tributary kingdom, Korea, was the powder keg for the inevitable clash between the two Asian empires – tired, ramshackle China and ambitious, modernizing Japan. In June 1894 Japan fomented an uprising in Seoul, and landed a force at Inchon. Clashes took place both by land and sea before war was declared on 1 August 1894; China shipped troops to the north and Japan to the south, but after defeats at Pyongyang on 15 September and at sea two days later the Chinese forces withdrew across the Yalu river. They were followed by the Japanese First Army in late October; Marshal Yamagata's advance was hampered by logistic problems, but the Japanese took Port Arthur in Fengtien province on 19 November.

The land war would involve some 150,000 Japanese troops, whose equipment and training outclassed those of, at most, 100,000 Chinese. China was unable to mobilize enough men or to transport them to the front lines, while the Japanese generals and admirals mostly cooperated effectively. On the same day that Port Arthur fell, Marshal Oyama's reinforced Third Army began landings on the Shantung peninsula, to capture the main Chinese naval base of Weihaiwei on 30–31 January. During 2–12 February the Japanese won a decisive naval victory off Weihaiwei. Beating off Chinese counter-attacks, First and Second armies advanced deeper into Manchuria, and after the general Sung Ch'ing's army was defeated at Tapingshan on 21–23 February Chinese resistance began to collapse. The Qing government sued for peace as the Japanese approached Peking, and the Treaty of Shimonoseki ended the war on 17 April 1895. Under its terms Japan gained Formosa and the Pescadores Islands, and China recognized Japan's proxy rule over a nominally independent Korea.

The Boxer Rebellion, 1900 This began as a popular revolt in Shantung province against the Qing regime, Chinese Christians and all foreigners, and spread rapidly. The killings of (in total) some 200 Western missionaries and perhaps 32,000 of their converts by the 'Boxers' – a movement so-called from their martial-arts training – spilled over into Chihli province. On 20 June the foreign legation quarter in Peking, defended by just over 400 troops from various nations, was brought under siege and attack. In an attempt to divert the Boxers' anger from the Qing monarchy the Dowager Empress allowed regular Imperial troops to assist the rebels. The legations held out for 55 days, while an international relief force nearly 19,000 strong was formed with contingents from Japan, Britain, the USA, France, Germany, Austro-Hungary, Russia and Italy. After defeating some 10,000 Chinese troops at Yang T'sun on 5–6 August this force relieved Peking on 15 August, and the Dowager Empress fled. That autumn, Russia occupied the remainder of Manchuria (a development that would lead directly to the Russo-Japanese War of 1904–05). In the aftermath of the rebellion the international troops sent out punitive columns around Peking until May 1901, killing thousands

1894: *Yung* 'braves' gather around their commander to be issued instructions as they bivouac for the night. Although this is a lithograph from a magazine it is accurate in its depiction of typical *Yung* uniform; the seated mandarin officer has a fur or fleece cloak and a slung sabre, and the soldiers wear bordered tabard-like surcoats with identification patches. The man on the left has a Dreyse M1841/48 'needle' rifle, as issued to a number of *Yung* units.

1900: the original caption describes this group as an honour guard. The five officers to the left show wide variations in uniform, with three types of headgear: the first and fifth from the left wear turbans, the second and third Manchu hats, and the fourth a silk skullcap. The jackets are of different designs, some having decorative panels and others being plain. The three soldiers on the right wear identical dark uniforms with turbans, plain tunics and trousers and Mongol-type boots; they are armed with Mauser rifles and have German belt equipment, the most commonly seen in service at this time.

of Chinese in often indiscriminate revenge. Helpless at the hands of the foreign powers, the Qing government had to agree in September 1901 to paying them an immense indemnity.

THE ARMIES

A 19th-century observer noted that 'There are Chinese troops; there is no Chinese Army – or rather, there are as many armies as there are regions.'

When fighting broke out between the British and Chinese during the First Opium War the Imperial Army was an enigma to the European powers. The Dynasty's total military manpower in 1840 is estimated at between 600,000 and 800,000 (rather than the 1,800,000 claimed at the time by the British government). Various Western sources calculated a figure of just over half a million troops, and one well-informed missionary wrote that there were between 30,000 and 36,000 soldiers in each of 18 provinces. Another source came to a similar total by claiming that small towns were garrisoned by approximately 40 soldiers, medium towns by 200, and large towns and cities by 2,000 men.

During the First Opium War the total number of troops actually mobilized to fight the British was quoted as 51,000. This force had to be raised by a levy of all the provinces, and many summoned from the furthest corners of the empire never arrived. Even troops in provinces neighbouring the seat of the conflict were said to have taken 30 to 40 days to reach the front line. On several occasions the army demonstrated an inability to mobilize troops at short notice. In one instance it took several days to get 6,000 men together in Peking to face a possible attack despite the fact that in theory there were several hundred thousand available in the locality.

From 1840 until the early 20th century the Imperial Army was divided into several distinct forces: the Army of the Eight Banners, the Army of the Green Standard, and, from the 1850s, the *Yung* militia armies.

Soldiers of the 'Ever Secure Army' parade at Ningpo in Chekiang province during the Taiping Rebellion. This 1,000-strong unit was originally raised in 1862 by a British naval officer employing Royal Marine cadres, but from the following year it was commanded by an American, James Cook. This was one of the more disciplined formations, along with the 'Ever Victorious Army' and the French-raised 'Ever Triumphant Army'. The men are neatly uniformed in dark blue jackets and trousers with green turbans, and wear crossbelt equipment; their weapons appear to be percussion-lock muskets of some type. In the summer the tunics were changed for light cotton garments more suitable for the Chinese heat.

Yunnanese troops photographed on the border with North Vietnam in 1890, five years after they had fought against the French. These tough-looking soldiers were responsible for keeping order in one of the most rebellious regions of the Chinese empire, and might find themselves fighting various irregulars and bandits. Most of the men have a uniform of sorts, with the usual black characters indicating their commander's name and their unit marked directly on their tunics. The officer in the centre and his second-in-command appear to be unarmed while the others have modern rifles, as well as pistols and knives tucked under their sashes and bandoliers.

The Army of the Eight Banners, 1840–1911

This was a force composed mainly of men of Manchurian background, the descendants of the Manchu invaders who had conquered China and set up the Qing Dynasty in 1644. Originally raised in 1601 in Manchuria, the army was initially organized in four 'Banners' *(pa-ch'i)* or corps; subsequently these were expanded, and finally each was divided in two, forming eight Banners. This enlarged force included a number of Han Chinese and Mongolian recruits, but the majority of 'Banner men' remained Manchurian, to a ratio of perhaps 3 to 1. The Eight Banners were a highly traditional force, in which skills such as archery were valued over more modern military training. Often units from different Banners were dispersed throughout China, in garrisons made up of mixed forces. The total number of Banner men appears to have remained fairly constant throughout the 19th century; in the 1860s the organization was said to total 250,000 soldiers, while at the start of the Sino-Japanese War in 1894 overall strength was recorded as 266,872.

Officially, the composition of a Banner corps was three divisions, each division *(kusai)* of five battalions, each battalion *(julan* or *cha-la*, in Manchu or Chinese respectively) with 1,500 men in five 300-man companies *(niru* or *tso-ling)*. In reality the strengths of Banner divisions and units varied greatly, and companies might be as small as 150 or even 50 men. Any formation of 3,000 Banner men or more was commanded by a general, units of 1,000 by a deputy lieutenant-general, and smaller units by a commandant.

The Green Standard Battalions (Lu-Ying), 1840–1911

This was a locally raised Han Chinese paramilitary force of 18 provincial armies responsible for keeping the peace, and although counted in the establishment of the Imperial Army few of its men received much military training. In 1851 its strength was said to be 516,000 infantry and 87,100 cavalry, plus 7,400 officers. By 1880 the total was estimated at 650,000 men; the reality, according to eyewitnesses, was that only some 50,000 of this number had received training and were armed with 19th-century firearms. At the outbreak of the Sino-Japanese War in 1894 Japanese intelligence gave the Green Standard armies a total strength of 599,019 men.

According to the original caption these are Imperial troops photographed in Korea in 1894. Few units fighting in the chaotic first Sino-Japanese campaign in Korea would have been as well turned-out as these men, with their light-coloured tunics and Manchu hats, and they may well be a bodyguard unit for one of the Imperial generals. They are drilling smartly, armed with Martini-Henry or Peabody-Martini rifles.

These troops were classed as either garrison infantry (most of them), infantry, or cavalry, and were generally formed into nominally 500-man battalions, though actual strength could vary between 50 and 1,000, and in emergencies they were made up by hasty conscription of any manpower available. For military campaigns several battalions were assembled into a regiment (*hsieh*) or brigade (*piao*) of varying strengths. Each provincial governor had at least one Green Standard battalion at his disposal, but might have up to a maximum of 5,000 men. The widely fragmented organization was deliberate, to prevent any regional magnate amassing too much strength, and it greatly diminished the military value of the whole. The Qing government made some attempts to improve the capabilities of the Green Standard armies; some units were given more rigorous training and better weaponry, and the title *Lian-jun* or 'trained armies' to signify their status. However, the vast majority of Green Standard troops were not much better than an untrained rabble, with few rifles and little artillery.

Some of the better elements within the Lu-Ying were eventually absorbed into the New Army (see below). Other units were allowed to continue to exist as a reserve for the army until the 1911 Revolution.

The Brave Battalions *(Yung-Ying)*, c.1860–1911

Because the Imperial Army proved incapable of dealing with the Taiping and Nien rebellions in the 1850s–60s, new regional military forces emerged. These 'armies' were basically local volunteers who wanted to defend their communities from marauding rebels, and were usually raised by local gentry and other leaders who had the confidence of the population. Known as *Yung* or 'braves', these volunteers were formed into *Yung-Ying* or 'Brave Battalions', usually led by a charismatic leader. Commanders of the Yung-Ying often built a command system around their own extended family in order to guarantee loyalty (which further weakened the Dynasty's grip over these forces). The only type of unit was the 500-strong battalion, and the number of these fluctuated as armies expanded and contracted. Although not well trained, they were usually well armed, with a higher percentage of modern rifles than other Imperial units.

By the end of the 1860s the estimated total of Yung troops was 300,000 men. The main Yung armies were the remnants of the old Hunan Army, the *Hsiang-chun*; the resurrected Hunan Army, the *Chu-chun*, under the command of Tso Tsung-t'ang; and the Anhwei Army, *Huai-chun*, under Li Hung-chang. Other smaller armies included the Honan Army, *Yu-chun*; the Shantung Army, *Tung-chun*; the Yunnan Army, *Tien-chun*; and the Szechwan Army, *Ch'uan-chun*.

The Hsiang Army or *Hsiang-chun* was recruited exclusively in Hunan province from 1853 onwards in order to fight the Taiping rebels. It differed from previous armies in having a permanent and parochial command system; officers were known as 'fathers', non-commissioned officers as 'younger brothers', and ordinary soldiers as 'sons'. By 1856 it had grown to 60,000 men, all from Hunan, but this number doubled over the next few years, and by 1860 there were 160,000 men under the direct command of its general, Tseng Kuo-fan. Some of these troops were recruited outside the province, but the officers were still 83 per cent Hunanese, many being related to or friends of the commanders. Attempts were made to modernize the Hsiang-chun, including the formation by 1864 of special squads in each battalion who were armed with modern rifles.

The Huai Army or *Huai-chun* was formed in Anhwei in 1861, again to fight the Taipings, and was commanded by Li Hung-chang. (Named the following year as acting governor of Kiangsu province, in 1870–95 this mandarin would become the most prominent Chinese statesman of the late 19th century, as governor-general of the capital province Chihli and an influential figure at the Qing court.) When the Taiping and Nien-fu rebellions were finally defeated in 1868 the Huai-chun was 70,000 strong. Due to the large number of cavalry employed by the Nien the mounted element of the Huai-chun had been increased to 17,000 men, and by 1868 these were organized into 29 battalions. The Huai Army developed many new ideas during campaigns against the Taipings, including the establishment of a river force or *Huai-Yang*; this was a marine corps that fought along the Yangtze and other rivers, transported by its own fleet of junks.

The Huai Army continued to exist until the Sino-Japanese War, although it lost much of its reputation over the years. It had been under-funded by the government, who feared its power, and Li Hung-chang's grip on his army had loosened as he aged. Some 26,000 Huai troops in 41 battalions each of 500 men fought in the 1894–95 war, but China's heavy defeat effectively ended the influence of all the Yung armies.

Modernized armies, 1894–1903

Even while the Imperial Army was being soundly defeated by the Japanese in 1894–95, attempts were being made to create modernized formations.

These soldiers seen in the southern port of Canton in 1902 belong to one of the *Yung-Ying* or 'Brave Battalions'. It was very unusual to see even a small group wearing identical uniforms, and the pristine appearance of their turbans, tunics, trousers and puttees suggests that they are in parade dress. Note the large black characters embroidered on their silk jackets. They are all armed with Austrian-designed 11mm Kropatschek M1878 rifles, a magazine-fed conversion of the Gras M1874 that had been ordered by the French Navy.

Cadets posing with their young officer – note his cuff bands of rank – at some date in the first few years of the 20th century. Their uniform is representative of the newly modernized 'armies' that were then being formed locally, often uniformed and armed independently by their commanders. Many units adopted the straw 'boater' sun hat as an alternative to the Manchu hat or turban worn previously; the silk shirts and trousers mimic Western uniform styles, and would soon be replaced with closer copies. European leather equipment was often delivered along with the rifles that were imported in large numbers; here the belly-pouch resembles the French M1869, so the rifles may be 11mm Chassepot M1866s.

(The generic Chinese term 'armies' was used, but in the Western sense they varied between divisional, corps, and true army strength.) The first, formed in 1894 at the suggestion of a German advisor named Von Hanneken, was known as the 'Pacification Army' or *Dingwu-Jun*, and was raised near Tientsin. By November 1895 it had reached a strength of 5,000 men in ten battalions.

A much larger force formed at about the same time was the 'Self Strengthening Army' raised at Nanking under the command of Chang Chih-tung, who had 35 German military advisors. Within this army of 60,000 men they helped to train a 20,000-strong elite force, organized along modern lines in units of infantry, cavalry, artillery and engineers. Other modernized armies formed at the end of the century included the 'Resolute Army' and the 'Tenacious Army', each with about 10,000 men and raised from Yung 'braves'. The 'Tiger Spirit Division' *Hu Shen-ying*, was formed in 1899; also with 10,000 men, this was among the forces defending Peking during the Boxer Rebellion.

With 40,000 infantry, cavalry and artillery in five divisions, the Guards Army or *Wu Wei-chun*, also formed in 1899, was the most potent force in northern China. Included as one of its divisions was the Pacification Army, formed five years earlier (see above), now commanded by Yuan Shi-kai. The rest of the Guards Army was made up of elements of the Tenacious Army, the Resolute Army, and the 10,000-strong Kansu Braves, the latter being a Yung formation recruited in the western Chinese provinces which enjoyed something of a wild reputation. The Guards Army suffered heavy casualties during the Boxer Rebellion, and was reduced to two divisions after 1900; when the Qing government then attempted to create a truly modern army (see below) it used Yuan Shi-kai's surviving division from the Guards Army as the nucleus.

As part of the modernization programmes introduced late in the century, 35 military schools were opened to train officers. A large number of military cadets would also be sent for training in Japan, most of them later becoming officers in the New Army.

The New Army (*Lu-Chun*), 1901–11

In the aftermath of the Boxer Rebellion in 1901 the Qing government issued a decree calling for the total reorganization of all existing Chinese armies into a modern unified force. The formation of this 'New Army' or *Lu-Chun* began in earnest in 1903, but at first the various formations were recruited on a regional basis, which led to the usual lack of standardization in unit size, arms and equipment. In December 1903 a government commission established the criteria for the formation of a modern regular army, and by 1905 six regular divisions had been established in northern China. The total strength of the New Army was estimated at 100,000 men, of whom 60,000 were stationed in the north.

Qing officials were dissatisfied by the pace of the army's growth, however, and in April 1906 a ten-year plan was introduced to create 36 divisions, to be uniformly trained and equipped. By the time of the 1911 Revolution only 14 of these divisions had been established, along with 2 brigades and 18 mixed brigades. In addition, a 10,000-strong Imperial Guard had been formed in 1908, at first recruited only from the Manchu population but accepting Han Chinese from 1910. With a total strength of 190,000 men by 1911, the New Army was nevertheless only a minority of the Chinese military establishment, though it received 50 per cent of the total military budget.

Official divisional strength in the New Army was 12,512 men with 54 artillery pieces: 12 infantry battalions totalling 6,924 men; 3 cavalry squadrons totalling 814 troopers; 2 artillery battalions with 882 men and 36 guns, plus a mountain artillery battalion of 453 men with 18 guns; an engineer battalion with 577 men; and a transport battalion of 573 men. The total number of officers throughout the division was 748, and the rest of the total was made up by 44 bandsmen and some 1,328 porters and labourers.

In addition to the New Army there were still a large number of provincial militia units called *Hsun-Fang-tui*. The more 'traditional' soldiers who made up this force were not as well trained as the New Army, but were more loyal to the Qing Dynasty. Although they received better training and rifles than other militia, the Hsun-Fang-tui were no match for regular units. In 1911 they reportedly totalled 277,000 men distributed throughout China, with a small artillery force of 46 guns in the Peking region. There was also a 54,621-strong remnant of Green Standard troops scattered across some provinces, though these were of negligible military value.

These recruits training on a parade ground near Peking in 1903 may well belong to the former Guards Army or *Wu Wei-chun*. Though reduced to two divisions after losses suffered during the Boxer Rebellion, it remained a vital force for the protection of the capital, and the division commanded by Yuan Shi-kai provided a nucleus for the New Army. These troops are wearing skullcaps and padded cotton uniforms with Mongol boots, and have been issued Mauser Gewehr 88 rifles and full field equipment.

CHARACTER OF THE IMPERIAL ARMY

Throughout the period covered by this book the Imperial Army was blighted by wholesale corruption, which affected every aspect of its organization and performance. Senior officers were described as more like 'army contractors' than field commanders; they drew a fixed sum of money from the government to run their army, and then used it however they wished – with predictable consequences. In 1894 many troops had not been paid for between three and five months, and at the outbreak of war with Japan there were many desertions. Often desertions and casualties actually benefited officers, who continued to draw money to pay the wages of these 'phantom' troops. For the same reason officers

often gave their men 'indefinite leave', sending them back to their villages while pocketing their pay. One of the most flagrant abuses involved an officer who in 1899 claimed to command 10,000 men. When he was investigated it turned out that the total under his command was about 800 troops; if his formation was ever inspected he simply hired enough coolies for the day to fill the parade ground.

Other reasons for weak performance included poor or non-existent training, outdated weaponry and tactics, and blind arrogance amongst the high command. Chinese officers genuinely believed that their army was superior to all others, and most officers and their men were resistant to any modernization. Chinese civilians were also strongly wedded to traditional ideas; it was known for officers to keep any better-trained and modern-armed troops in barracks, while the men they sent out to drill in public carried only spears and bows so as to avoid provoking any popular uproar.

To the frustration of foreign advisors, many Chinese soldiers had a negative attitude to the modern weapons they were given in the mid- to late 19th century. This puzzling disregard often led to actual abuse of their muskets and rifles, for instance by removing the sights, whose purpose they seemed not to understand. Others sawed off the breech or muzzle of their weapons for no apparent reason, and allowed them to get bent or dented. An account from Vietnam suggests that some troops were more interested in the supposedly intimidating noise made by firearms than in their accuracy. During the Sino-Japanese War many soldiers were said to be 'wary' of their new breech-loading rifles and said they preferred the old types which they knew how to fire, while being

Imperial Army senior officers watch their troops taking part in training manoeuvres in 1904, their appearance typifying the conservatism that had long prevented China from mounting any effective resistance to Western and Japanese incursions. In cold weather they wear cloth earmuffs attached to their Manchu hats, which have metal 'pommel' decorations at the apex and trailing peacock feathers denoting their mandarin ranks.

Imperial troops photographed in March 1895 with their officer (right), during the fighting for the port of Yingkow in Fengtien province in the last stage of the Sino-Japanese War. The combat of Tianzhuangtai in which these men are about to take part was a small-scale but vicious encounter; the Japanese gave no quarter, and Western observers reported that most of the Chinese wounded had been killed by having their throats cut. Most of these soldiers carry the 15ft-long bamboo spears with which they were supposed to protect the musketeers during reloading, exactly as on a 17th-century European battlefield. Soldiers like these could not be expected to stand for long against Japanese troops with modern rifles. (Chinese Historical Photographs Project)

'afraid to shoot from these new ones' (perhaps because of their greater kick). This led to a Chinese policy of never scrapping older rifles and muskets when new ones were issued; obviously, this use of weapons dating back to the early 1800s caused chaos when it came to issuing ammunition (see below, 'Weapons').

These and other weaknesses of the Imperial Army were fully brought into focus by its total defeat at Japanese hands in 1894–95. Western correspondents related a series of tragi-comic stories about the Chinese Army, which are no less revealing for being couched in racist terms. (One even claimed that an Imperial Army general had issued his troops with bags of pepper to throw in the faces of Japanese troops, with the idea that while they were sneezing the Chinese spearmen could rush forward and kill them.)

While the individual Chinese soldier was often brave, the performance of units in battle naturally depended upon the quality of their officers; if they lacked good leadership units tended to panic, and often fled the battlefield. In some cases the fleeing troops were rallied by an able officer and would then stand and fight, often to the last man. Both these tendencies are vividly confirmed by eyewitness accounts of actions between Kwangsi and French troops in Tonkin in 1884–85. The brutal truth was that an outdated army, poorly led, poorly armed and poorly trained, was bound to fail against the modern European and Japanese armies that it increasingly faced during this period.

Foreign advisors

In an attempt to address the weakness of the Imperial Army an increasing number of foreign military advisors and instructors were employed by the Qing Dynasty. Some arrived as part of official military missions, while many others were employed in small numbers by individual military governors of provinces. During the Taiping Rebellion a number of foreign adventurers found themselves in command of Imperial units, and from 1860 several foreigners were invited by the Qing government to help establish new formations and recruit Chinese volunteers.

Such units were usually officered by Western soldiers of fortune who

A rather unkempt-looking Imperial soldier pictured in Mongolia in the summer of 1907, guarding a foreign mission to this Chinese dependency (note the European in the background, wearing a white pith helmet). The cotton uniform consists of a locally made sun hat, a shirt, loose-fitting trousers and cloth shoes. His weapon is unidentified, but the cartridge bandolier that appears to be his sole item of equipment confirms that it is a breech-loader.

This line of soldiers in Szechwan province in 1899 apparently belong to one of the newly raised modernized units, wearing dark uniforms and the straw 'boaters' increasingly seen from 1895 onwards. The weapons are not identifiable here, but even at this date they may be elderly US Springfield percussion rifle-muskets.

In 1860, elite Manchu troops of one of the Banner formations take part in target practice in preparation for war against British and French armies that were equipped with the latest rifled firearms accurate out to 300 yards. This mixture of bows and matchlocks in the same unit was seen in the Imperial armies as late as 1894.

found themselves unemployed after military service in their own armies. An American civilian, Frederick T. Ward, was employed to raise the so-called 'Ever Victorious Army' in 1860. Originally a 200-strong mercenary force of Americans, British and other Europeans, in 1861 the EVA was converted into a larger Chinese force with foreign officers. Reaching a strength of 4,000–5,000 men after Ward's death, it came under the command of the British engineer officer LtCol Charles Gordon, later to gain fame in the Sudan; previously serving with the British garrison at Tientsin, Gordon was seconded at the request of Li Hung-chang. Although the EVA was clearly a better-than-average formation that fought in many engagements, its role in the overall defeat of the Taiping Rebellion has been overstated.

In 1872 the US government even suggested sending Gen Emory Upton, a Civil War hero and respected military theoretician, to reorganize the Imperial Army according to 'the principles of modern science and economy', but the proposal was quietly forgotten when the US ambassador reported the full extent of the army's chaos and corruption. Although there was no large-scale involvement of foreigners, reports of the employment of small numbers of advisors continued. For instance, two English instructors were reported to be training a modern rifle unit in Amoy in 1875, and in 1880 a number of British and French officers were said to be training Imperial troops. The efforts of these instructors often turned out to be futile, however, since they were used unwisely by the Chinese. Eyewitnesses wrote that instead of being allowed to teach modern tactical skills the instructors were often relegated to the role of 'drill sergeants' which could have been performed just as easily by Chinese officers. By the late 19th century the hands-on role of foreign advisors with combat units was in any case being reduced; most Europeans were now employed in military academies, arsenals and armouries, where their technical skill could be utilized without hurting Chinese military pride.

After China's defeat in the Sino-Japanese War the employment of foreign advisors increased once again. In 1896 the Qing government employed a German officer, Col Liebert, with 20 other instructors. Li Hung-chang recruited Europeans according to their national reputations, employing French cavalry instructors, German gunnery experts and British naval officers. In the first few years of the 20th century a number of Japanese military advisors even went to China, including in 1902 MajGen Yamani; in 1905 two Japanese advisors were reportedly active in Shantung province, and in 1907 the Viceroy of Hankow had a number of others. Not all Japanese advisors were highly rated, however, with those in Hankow described by eyewitnesses as being of poor quality. Whatever the quality of the foreign instructors and advisors, their work was frequently wasted. Once their contracts were up and they returned home, it was often far too easy for the Imperial Army officers and their men to return to their bad habits.

WEAPONS

Infantry weapons, 1840–95

Most of the weaponry carried by the Imperial Chinese Army in 1840 had been in use for many centuries. Spears, halberds, billhooks, tridents and other polearms were the commonest weapons. In the best units these might be beautifully made and highly decorated, while the majority were crudely produced in local smithies. The use of these archaic types of weapon decreased during the course of the 19th century, but even in images of the 1894–95 Japanese War the majority of Chinese troops are shown carrying them, and at least one unit still had halberds in 1903.

Swords of various types were used, those issued to the common soldiers having straight blades (and corruption even led to some soldiers being issued with useless tin-plate swords). Better-quality weapons carried by officers included curved sabres such as the *piandao* ('slicing sabre'), the *niuweidao* ('oxtail sabre'), and the *yenmaidao* ('goose-quill sabre'). Throughout the period irregular soldiers were reportedly armed with crude weapons such as flails, cudgels, and farming implements like hoes.

Missile weapons included crossbows and composite reflex bows, the latter being the chosen weapon of the elite Manchu class; archery was a highly valued skill among their Banner men even after the advent of modern firearms. The only firearms employed in any numbers in 1840 were matchlock muskets, which had been introduced into China by the Portuguese in the 16th century, and which remained in Imperial Army service well into the middle decades of the 19th century. Examples of matchlocks captured in the 1840s included some that had been mass-produced in government arsenals; these were well made, with a series of strengthening rings around the barrel. Even when relatively modern smoothbore and rifled muskets were imported the matchlock long remained the most common firearm.

The Ever Victorious Army was one of the first Chinese forces to buy in European and US weaponry. The main rifled firearms purchased for the EVA were Sharps M1863 breech-loading percussion carbines, along with British Tower M1851 and M1853 muzzle-loading muskets, and Colt Dragoon and Navy revolvers. Other Imperial armies bought Enfield P1853 and P1857 muzzle-loading percussion rifle-muskets, as well as the Snider breech-loading conversion of the Enfield. By the 1860s most Imperial armies had modern rifle units, and the consequently growing demand for such weapons was met by sometimes unscrupulous arms dealers who supplied second- and even third-hand weapons from Europe.

Amongst the better purchases were large numbers of Dreyse M1841/48 'needle' rifles, which were issued to some units in the 1870s. By that decade

This classic 1871 photograph by John Thomson shows a Manchu matchlock man of the Imperial Army. The matchlock used by the Chinese in the 19th century was only slightly modified from the original type introduced by Portuguese traders in the 16th century. Like the Japanese version, it had a short buttstock that often was not pulled tight into the shoulder for firing, further limiting its already short accurate range. Note the waist bandolier of bottle-like bamboo 'cartridges' containing measured powder charges.

Artillerymen of the Ningpo Field Force photographed on a training ground in the 1870s with their muzzle-loading brass cannon. When the Ever Victorious Army was decommissioned after the crushing of the Taiping Rebellion a remnant of it was retained at Ningpo in Chekiang province, where it was instructed by the Australian Maj J.C. Watson and the English Col Cook. In the 1870s this force was a well-drilled 150-strong company with an attached three-gun battery (though each of a different calibre). These gunners have smart uniforms differing only in the positioning of the dark-coloured identification patches on their jackets (the patches may well have been issued to soldiers to be sewn on individually). Later this force was given a European-style uniform similar to that worn by the Ever Victorious Army (see Plate B2); this had a green turban, a dark blue tunic with green facings in winter, and a white tunic with blue facings in summer.

large-scale importation of single-shot breech-loaders in 11mm calibre had begun. These included the French Gras M1874 rifle and carbine, the US-designed Remington 'rolling block', and Mauser M1871 and Steyr rifles from Germany and Austria. In 1876 the Imperial government placed an order for 26,000 M1871s, and in 1880 it decided to try to standardize on this model, which was purchased steadily from then on.

Since 1864–65 the Chinese government had been producing their own copies of modern firearms in several small arsenals, which also produced a variety of swords and other military accoutrements. However such small-scale production was never going to be sufficient to meet the needs of the modernizing Imperial Army. For instance, the Shanghai arsenal was producing copies of the Remington rifle in the 1880s, but only at a rate of ten per day. An arsenal established by Li Hung-chang in Shanghai in 1865 would also produce copies of the Remington, but their quality was so poor that even Li's own troops refused them.

Not all new arsenals produced modern weaponry, and one that opened in 1862 in Anqing produced both matchlocks and *jingals*. The latter was a popular class of weapon among the Chinese, being an oversized version of a musket or rifle for mounting on a rest or as a rampart gun. Up to 9ft long and crewed by two men, jingals took up to 4 minutes to reload. The Chinese persisted in using these cumbersome weapons, and continued producing them in their arsenals well after the turn of the century. The Canton arsenal used Remington and Spencer rifles as the basis, fitted with 6ft-long barrels of 1in calibre. Although the manager of the arsenal conceded that the guns were too long for normal use, he countered that they were 'impressive' in appearance – a revealing comment on the Chinese relationship with firearms.

Even with the importation and domestic production of many muskets and rifles by the 1880s the Chinese were still poorly armed. In 1884 an Austrian expert visiting China noted that 50 per cent of the Imperial soldiers issued with firearms were armed with 'ancient-looking' matchlocks; 75 per cent of the remainder had muzzle-loading muskets from Europe and the USA; and the other 25 per cent had modern breech-loaders from a variety of sources. Many Chinese units in 1894 had up to 20 different types of musket and rifle in service, leading to logistical chaos. One eyewitness present with a unit fighting during the Sino-Japanese War described mixed-up cartridges for the unit's various rifles piled loosely on the floor. As each soldier approached the pyramid of ammunition he picked up a handful of rounds to see if they would fit his rifle; if they didn't, he would simply throw them back on the pile so that the next soldier could try his luck.

Artillery, 1840–95

It is impossible to estimate how many artillery pieces were in service in the Imperial Chinese Army between 1840 and 1895, but it can be said with confidence that a large number of them were museum pieces of steadily diminishing value in modern warfare.

In 1840 the artillery in use included cannon and mortars made from a wide variety of metals including brass, copper and iron, some of them more than a century old. No guns seem ever to have been decommissioned, no matter their age, and crews often took their lives in their hands when firing some of them. Cannon used in the defence of fortresses were mounted on fixed wooden platforms with only a system of wedges to alter elevation. When they needed to be moved into battle they would be mounted on gun carriages which were often crudely made. The Chinese were not really interested in using their artillery for counter-battery work, and when in the field their guns were usually sited where the enemy was expected to advance. In 1844 a British correspondent described three guns captured in an engagement three years earlier. These were a brass 4-pdr which was 6ft long; an 'immense' and heavily decorated brass 12-pdr which was 11ft long; and a 'silk gun' – a small brass gun wrapped around tightly with silk cloth and cat gut.

From the 1850s the Imperial Army did import muzzle-loaders from the West, and often employed foreign instructors to train them in their use. These included various 'Napoleon' field pieces such as the M1857 in 6-pdr and 12-pdr calibres, as well as some rifled muzzle-loaders. Copies of the former types would have been relatively easy to cast in local arsenals, and were presumably used alongside imported weapons.

In the latter years of the century the Imperial Army imported more modern guns from the European powers; for example, in 1880 Krupp delivered to China 150 siege and fortress guns along with 275 field guns. As with other weaponry, however, the Imperial troops were often reluctant to accept modern artillery into service. As late as the 1880s, and despite the best efforts of German, French and British instructors, many Chinese artillerymen preferred older smooth-bore guns to the brand-new Krupps.

Infantry weapons, 1895–1911

As the Dynasty attempted to modernize its army after defeat in 1894–95 large numbers of small arms were imported, and copies of new rifles and

With their Mauser Gewehr 88 rifles stacked, an apparently well-armed and well-uniformed unit of Revolutionary troops gather at a railway station in 1911. They appear to wear Imperial dark blue uniforms stripped of all insignia, and may belong to a former Imperial unit that has joined the anti-Qing forces *en bloc*, which occurred in many New Army divisions. When faced with opponents like these, some less well-equipped and trained Imperial units were demoralized enough either to change sides themselves, or simply to desert.

revolvers were also made in Chinese arsenals. The Imperial Army placed huge orders for rifles with most of the European manufacturers; for example, in 1899 an order was placed with Germany for 460,000 Mauser rifles and 3 million cartridges. In 1897 the Russian government, in an effort to raise some revenue, offered the Chinese 500,000 Berdan rifles at a very competitive price of 7 *taels* each and with five years' interest-free credit. In August 1903 the powerful general Yuan Shi-kai placed orders for 23,000 rifles, 48 field guns and 50 machine guns for his New Army division. Press reports from 1907 also claimed that a German firm had received an order for no fewer than 2 million rifles. One of the last pre-Revolution orders for the New Army in 1908 was for thousands of Japanese 6.5mm Arisaka magazine rifles and carbines. Any new rifles were added to the multitude of types already in service, different models being mixed even within single units.

One important commentator on this chaotic process was the British Rear Adml Charles Beresford, who in 1898 was asked by the Qing court to inspect the Imperial Army: 'During my visit to the different armies I counted in the ranks fourteen different rifles. Three different patterns of Mauser rifles, Martini-Henrys, Winchester repeaters, Mannlichers, Remingtons, Peabody-Henrys, Sniders, Enfields, Tower Muskets and Berdans'. He also mentioned muzzle- and breech-loading jingals between 9ft and 10ft long.

Machine guns

Like most military powers in the late 19th century the Chinese investigated the possibilities of quick-firing multi-barrelled guns and machine guns. The first they purchased were a few Belgian-made Montigny M1863 *mitrailleuse* hand-cranked multi-barrel guns. General Jung Hung acted as an agent for

the Gatling company, and under his influence a number of their guns were bought. The Chinese also purchased 151 of the Maxim-Nordenfelt M1889 between 1892 and 1895. By 1900 the Chinese government had purchased 207 Maxim and Vickers machine guns from Britain; later Maxim imports included five of the M1901 and a single M1906.

The Imperial government also began to reverse-engineer some of these weapons and to produce them in Chinese arsenals. From 1890 the Tianjin arsenal produced Maxim machine guns and the multi-barrelled Nordenfelt, and two years later the Nanking arsenal could produce Maxim and Hotchkiss machine guns and Nordenfelts. By 1910 machine guns were being produced at both the Kaifeng and Tsinan arsenals, and the Maxim M1909 was being made at the Chengtu arsenal. In the last few years before the Revolution the Chinese purchased six of the German Bergmann M1910, and ordered 50 of the Austro-Hungarian Skoda M1909; however, only 20 of the Skodas were delivered before the outbreak of the Revolution, the rest being impounded by the Austro-Hungarian government in 1914.

A Maxim machine-gun crew training under the watchful eye of a European civilian, presumably a representative from the manufacturers. When this photograph was taken in the early 1900s machine guns were often mounted on wheeled artillery-style carriages; note the ponies in the background carrying ammunition boxes. A Chinese commission had at first rejected buying machine guns because of the cost of their huge expenditure of ammunition, but this decision was soon rescinded, and by 1900 the Imperial Army had bought more than 200 Maxim and Vickers guns from Britain.

Artillery, 1895–1911
During the Imperial Army's attempts to modernize around the turn of the century it bought artillery from several nations. Between 1895 and 1900 the Chinese purchased from British companies 71 fortress guns and 123 field guns of various types. At the time of the Boxer Rebellion the Chinese had received 8.7cm Krupp M1886 field guns as well as 12cm and 15cm breech-loaders from the same factory. In 1900 the Chinese ordered a total of 200 Krupp mountain guns, and some of the 7cm L/14 model were delivered to the Imperial Army. Other mountain guns purchased

The crew of a medium field gun of the Imperial Army photographed during the battle for Hankow in Hupeh province, 1911; they wear the light khaki cotton summer version of the 1904 uniform, apparently with 1911 rank patches on their collars. By the time of the Revolution the Imperial Army had almost 1,000 modern guns in service: 372 field pieces and 600 mountain guns, mostly of German and British types but with some French, Austrian and Japanese. These were fielded by 162 batteries, which were unevenly distributed through the Army's divisions.

included small quantities of both the Austro-Hungarian 72.5mm Skoda M1907 and the French 75mm Schneider M1907. Other field guns in Imperial Army service included the Japanese 75mm Arisaka and French Schneider-Canet and Schneider-Creusot rifled cannon. In 1910 the Chinese purchased an additional 55 7.5cm Krupp field guns to equip the expanding artillery of the Imperial Guard. As with other Imperial Army weapons purchases, the different types of artillery in service led to a mix of pieces within formations; even in the elite 1st Division of the New Army Japanese and German field and mountain guns were divided between the nine batteries.

(Continued on page 33)

Revolutionary soldiers manning a light mountain gun during the fighting for Hankow. According to accounts of this battle these light guns were no match for the Imperial Army's howitzers, and most of the Revolutionary gunners were killed. These volunteers are wearing black or dark blue Imperial uniforms stripped of insignia, and the man at the left is armed with a Mauser Gewehr 88 rifle.

IMPERIAL ARMY, 1840s–60s
1: Cavalry bowman, Eight Banners Army, 1840–41
2: Halberdier, Tsung Kuo-fen's Army, 1856
3: Mathclock man, Mongolian Left Banner, 1860

2

3

1

A

B

STANDARD-BEARERS, 1850s–80s

1: Ever Victorious Army, 1864
2: Tiger man, Yeh Ming'chen's Army; Canton, 1857
3: Kwantung Victorious Army, 1885
4 & 5: Yung-ying standards, late 19th C

CHINESE BORDER TROOPS, 1870s–80s
1: Tso Tsung-t'ang's Army, Kansu, 1872
2: Yunnan auxiliary, Tang Ching-sung's Army, 1884
3: Black Flags standard-bearer, Tonkin, 1884

C

D

E

MODERNIZED ARMIES, 1900–08
1: Cavalryman, General Ma's Army; Manchuria, 1904
2: Rifleman, Mei Tung-yu's Army; Tientsin, 1902
3: Rifleman, Vanguard of Right Division; Shantung, 1903

IMPERIAL ARMY, 1908–11
1: General, parade uniform, 1908
2: Cavalryman, Imperial Guard, 1910
3: Infantryman, Tibet, 1910

1911 REVOLUTION
1: ColSgt, infantry, New Army
2: Volunteer, Revolutionary Army
3: Standard-bearer, Revolutionary Army

UNIFORMS & EQUIPMENT

1840–1900

Over the 70-year period covered by this book Chinese uniforms changed dramatically, and it seems sensible to divide our descriptions between the 19th and 20th centuries. In the pages that follow we also cross-refer to the colour plates.

Chinese Imperial soldiers in the mid- to late 19th century always wore brightly coloured uniforms. The main garment was a loose-fitting tunic of silk, cotton or linen, which was usually bordered in a contrasting colour to the body (see Plates A3, B1, B3, D1, D3 and E3.) The tunic was issued by the unit commander, but anything worn under it was usually provided by the soldiers themselves. On the chest and back of the tunic was a cloth disc, usually in white or yellow, which bore characters displaying information on the soldier's unit and commander (see below, 'Identification patches'). Although tunics of just about any shade might be worn, the predominant colours were blue and red with contrasting borders. Often the tunic also had a decorative panel down the middle, again usually in a contrasting colour to the main body.

Many Western eyewitnesses left accounts of the different coloured tunics worn by the Imperial Army. White cotton tunics were seen in 1840, but in 1842 a unit of the Imperial Guard at Ningpo were 'sumptuously dressed in black and purple velvet'. In 1860 troops defending the approaches to the Taku Forts were wearing brilliant yellow uniforms, with silk standards of the same colour; one commentator pointed out drily that they certainly 'stood out from the foliage'. Banner troops generally wore tunics in the colours of their flags, with the 1st and 5th corps wearing yellow, the 2nd and 6th white, the 3rd and 7th red, and the 4th and 8th Banners blue. This was not always the case, however; in 1858 some wore brown tunics edged with pink, and yellow edged with black in 1860. At Bac Ninh in the Red river delta in 1884 an eyewitness noted troops (presumably from Kwangsi, but possibly from Yunnan) wearing

This lithograph from 1840 illustrates what are described as 'Tartar troops', or Manchu soldiers. Although heavily stylized, it does show the types of dress worn by the Imperial Army during the First Opium War. The horse-archers wear Manchu hats with a tassel attached to the crown and embroidered surcoats, while the infantry have plain black hats. In the centre background is a medieval-looking cavalryman wearing what was described as a 'hard metal helmet'.

blue uniforms edged in black green edged with dark red, and all-yellow silk. Troops defending Port Arthur from the Japanese in 1895 were seen wearing tunics in red, yellow, blue, and green.

Many troops wore a sleeveless surcoat or tabard over a loose long-sleeved smock, with the usual identification discs on front and back (see Plates A2, C2, C3 and E3). This type of garment appears from photographic evidence to have been more common among Yung units, who often displayed on it a single black Chinese character signifying 'courage' or 'bravery'.

Trousers for common soldiers were usually of loose-fitting cotton or silk and were worn with either white stockings or calf-length Mongol-type boots; leggings were also worn over these, hanging from a belt, as were puttees of various lengths. Footwear took the form of cloth slipper-type shoes with cardboard or felt soles in summer and wooden soles in winter. The Mongol-type boot was worn by many troops in winter, its quality depending on the status of the wearer. In summer soldiers in the south of China often wore straw sandals, and many poorer soldiers would have had to go barefoot, since most troops had to purchase their own footwear.

Typical headgear was usually either a turban worn in various styles (see Plates A2, B2, D3 and E2), or a Manchu hat. Most soldiers wore blue turbans but black and red ones were worn by regulars, and yellow, scarlet and dark blue ones were worn by some Yung units. The black Manchu hat with turned-up brim and red crown was made from various materials depending on rank (see Plates A1, A3, D1 and E1), and might have a stone or metal 'pearl' at the apex. Cavalrymen and artillerymen usually had two fur tails of squirrel, fox, mink, cat or other animal attached to the top 'pommel' of the hat and hanging down at the back. Other headgear included sun hats of bamboo, rattan or straw in various sizes and styles (see Plates C2 and C3), often following patterns traditional in the soldiers' region of origin.

Military mandarins or officers wore a silk jacket in various colours but predominantly in purple. On the front and back of the jacket was a highly decorative embroidered cloth panel featuring various animal designs depending on the wearer's rank (see below, 'Ranks and insignia'). Headgear was a Manchu hat in winter and a bamboo sun hat in summer, both with red tassels attached to the top. Senior officers wore peacock feathers hanging down from the apex at the back, depending upon a complicated system of mandarin grades.

Identification patches

The main feature of most Imperial Army uniforms of the 19th and early 20th centuries was the white linen patch sewn to the chest and back of the soldier's tunic, jerkin, shirt or coat. Although the vast majority of these were circular some were square or oblong; a few circular patches were even seen in a smaller version sewn to the upper sleeves (see above).

These identification patches carried in Chinese characters a variety of information about the individual soldier, his unit and its commanders. Some carried the name or number of the individual soldier, his unit's name, and the name of its commanding officer or the army's commander-in-chief. They might show whether the wearer was a sentry-post leader, a bodyguard commander, or a member of the unit's front rank. Some of the discs were reported by Western observers to have 'boastful' inscriptions on them, but this may have been simply a mistranslation of standard characters worn by Yung units. One correspondent in 1894 says that the patches had either 'the ideograph for "brave", a rampant dragon, the initial of the wearer's commander, the monogram of his province, or a regiment or corps badge'.

This practice was ridiculed in the foreign press for giving the enemy an easy target to aim at. In support of this view, one commentator described an engagement between Japanese and Chinese troops that he had witnessed. He noted that 'the Japanese lay down on the ground and deliberately took aim at or just below this circle on the Chinaman's breast. They could see this even when the faces of their foes were not

These Imperial Army trumpeters of the late 1890s stand outside their barracks ready to summon their comrades to a parade or roll call; this type of trumpet was usually played by musicians at the head of a column or to encourage the troops in battle, and many European memoirists recalled being unnerved by the sound. The soldiers at left and right wear straw 'boaters' apparently with decorative bands. Unusually, three of these men have white cloth identification discs at their shoulders instead of the larger versions normally worn on the chest and back.
Note at centre the traditional Manchu hairstyle, drawn back into a long pigtail. By the first decade of the 20th century Army officers had varying attitudes towards the Qing Dynasty, and one sign of loyalty to the regime was the retention of the pigtail.

Imperial troops marching across the plains of northern China during the Russo-Japanese War in 1905, wearing typical wadded cotton winter uniforms and Mongol boots; note the surcoats with identification patches and contrasting-colour borders, and the tasselled plugs protecting the muzzles of their rifles from rain. During this war the Qing government in Peking was powerless to prevent Chinese territory being violated by both sides. It even turned a blind eye to the recruiting of Chinese irregulars; many fought as irregular cavalry on the side of the Japanese, and others were employed as auxiliaries by the Russians.

distinguishable … after the action all 22 of the Chinese wounded were found to have been hit below the waist' – 20 died of their wounds. Late in the 19th century it became more common to sew individual Chinese characters directly onto the front of the jacket (see Plate F3); these conveyed the same information, but did not provide such a conspicuou aiming-mark.

Winter uniforms

In the winter Imperial Army regular troops usually wore the same style of silk or cotton jacket but with additional linings sewn in (see Plate C1) Some seem to have been issued with padded versions of the summe tunic, but these were a minority. Others simply wore multiple layers o cotton uniform or civilian clothing underneath the tunic; one eyewitnes described soldiers as being 'swathed in several layers of blue cotto wadded clothing, giving them a rather balloon-type appearance' Although this kind of clothing would have been practical for, e.g., stati guard duty, it would have been somewhat restrictive in combat.

Some troops, especially in the north of China, wore fur or fleece coat over their standard uniform. Troops in the central provinces were issued with a sheepskin coat every three years, but those serving in the north were issued with up to eight each per year. Sheep- or yak-skin jerkins wer also worn over the cotton uniform, as were gloves when available. Winte headgear was usually a wadded cotton hat with earflaps that could b worn tied up on top or down over the ears; some were lined with fur o fleece, and they came in a wide variety of styles (e.g., Plates C1 and D2) Other soldiers had to make do by winding their turbans around the hea and face to form an improvised balaclava.

Equipment, 1840–1900

Equipment carried by the average Chinese soldier in the 19th centu was basic, with most relying on the unit's baggage train for their need

Also photographed in 1905, these Imperial cavalrymen wait to embark on a troop train. The troopers are wearing pale-coloured padded cotton tunics and trousers, with some kind of loose-fitting cloth cap (compare with Plate F1). Their shoulder straps appear to be in the white of the New Army's cavalry branch, and their equipment and carbines are probably Japanese. These uniforms do not entirely conform to the 1904 dress regulations, but they are practical in the Manchurian winter.

An Imperial officer poses in a studio at the time of the Sino-Japanese War, 1894–95 (compare with Plate E2). His Manchu hat has a trailing peacock feather indicating his status. His silk jacket could be in any dark colour, but blue was the most usual, with the facing nearly always in a contrasting colour. The three gold bands around the cuffs are modernized rank insignia.

Various cloth bags were carried for personal possessions, along with personal cooking-pots, pans and cups. Men armed with matchlock or imported flintlock muskets were sketched by eyewitnesses such as Lamprey with powder and ball in small bags and flasks hanging from cords; by the 1860s at latest, images also show fabric or leather waist bandoliers of plugged bamboo tubes for measured charges (see Plates A3 and C2), and R. Swinhoe's *Narrative of the North China Campaign of 1860* shows this in conjunction with a ceramic priming flask. One eyewitness in 1883 describes Imperial troops having 'white linen back packs and many canvas bandoliers round their necks and tied around the waist'. Many soldiers carried umbrellas, for protection from the sun and rain alike. Some also carried fans; on the march these might be arranged as sun shields by sticking the handle down the back of the jacket behind the neck, and securing it by winding the pigtail around it. Water flasks and bottles were also carried by some, but were far from universal. The only other habitual items of equipment were small wooden 'dog tags' hanging from belts, marked with characters identifying the soldier's name, grade of service, unit and formation.

Modernized uniforms, 1894–1911

As part of the modernization policy Imperial soldiers began to be issued with slightly more practical uniforms in this period. Tunics and trousers were still often made of silk but were more closely tailored and better suited to modern combat. While the old turban remained the main type of headgear (see Plate F3), several armies raised after 1894 began to use smaller straw hats like Western 'boaters' (see Plate F2), with brims of various widths. Many bore coloured hat bands, either matching the colour of the tunic or bearing white Chinese characters identifying the unit. Other forms of headgear introduced at about this time were various designs of peaked soft cap (e.g., Plate F1).

A Chinese Officer.

This photograph taken during the Imperial Army's grand manoeuvres in summer 1907 shows the haphazard modernization process of Chinese uniforms. These cavalrymen all wear loose-fitting tunics and trousers, with a new style of field cap – it does not look like the regulation 1904 model, but may be a local attempt to copy it. Note the large white-metal cap badge of the 1904 regulations, which showed a pearl centred on a circular dragon design.

Commanders of modernized units around the turn of the century tried to adapt their troops' clothing for increased practicality and a more up-to-date appearance (see Plates F1 and F3), but since these were issued locally on a unit-by-unit basis there was no such thing as a 'typical' uniform in this period. It is often presumed that by the time of the 1911 Revolution the majority of Imperial troops were wearing conventional 'Western' uniforms, but although most of the New Army divisions had clothed their men in the European fashion the vast majority of Chinese troops were still wearing older styles. Right up until the Revolution, Green Standard and Yung units were still seen wearing brightly coloured uniforms.

New Army uniforms and equipment, 1903–11

The uniforms worn by the New Army from 1903–04 were of modern Western styles, and the introduction of the 1904 dress regulations prescribed uniforms very similar to those worn by the European and Japanese armies. However, photographic evidence suggests that the actual issue of modern uniforms was piecemeal, with only the elite divisions receiving them before the Revolution. A series of dress regulations between 1904 and 1911 also contributed to the confused picture.

The 1904 regulations introduced Western-style dark blue winter and light khaki summer uniforms (see Plates G3 and H1 respectively). Unique light grey uniforms were prescribed for the Imperial Guard (see Plate G2), but these may not have been issued to all its soldiers before 1911. Rank insignia for other ranks changed several times during these seven years, with a new system being introduced in 1911 (see Plate H1) but rankers' uniforms otherwise seem to have remained unaltered. By contrast, officers' uniforms and ranks were in a constant state of flux leading to a confusing mix-and-match of caps, jackets and trousers that continued into the early Republican period (see MAA 463, *Chinese Warlord Armies 1911–30*).

Leather equipment worn by the Imperial Army at the turn of the century usually came from German sources, presumably being supplied along with the large quantities of Mauser rifles imported by the Chinese; German-supplied belts came with white-metal buckle-plates with an embossed dragon design. In 1909 the full equipment of the Imperial soldier was listed as: backpack, rubberized groundsheet, mess tin, small drinking can, two ammunition pouches, and a haversack. A rolled greatcoat was carried strapped to the backpack, and among its contents was a spare pair of shoes. Each soldier was also supposed to carry one of three tools – either a pick, a shovel or a hatchet.

Ranks and insignia, 1840–1911

The old Imperial rank or grade system for mandarins as used by senior military officers was shown by the wearing of highly decorated cloth panels on the front of their robes. Each of these grade squares featured its own animal to symbolize the wearer's rank: 1st grade, the mythical *qulin*; 2nd grade, lion; 3rd grade, leopard; and 4th grade, tiger. Although there were also more junior 5th to 9th grades of mandarin their insignia were not worn by military officers. Below mandarin rank the junior officers and other ranks had titles such as *fu-shao-kuan*, assistant company commander; *shih-chang*, sergeant/leader of ten men; *hao-ling*, courier; and *chang ping*, common soldier. These titles were written on the identification discs on the front and back of the tunic.

In the 1890s a new Westernized rank system was displayed on the cuffs of the silk tunic to replace the mandarins' rank squares (see Plate E2). This system used a series of 1–3 black or yellow bands below 1–3 round buttons, although in some photographs of junior officers the button is absent. Officially, 1 button and 1–3 bands identified 2nd lieutenant,

A group of Imperial cadets from Yuan Shi-kai's New Army pose for a photograph in a Berlin studio while attending artillery, engineer and other technical courses; Yuan was determined to build his army into the most modern and powerful in China. Neither of these European-style mounted troops' uniforms conform to any Chinese dress regulation, so they are presumably privately designed and tailored. Most officers came from the highest classes of Qing society, so would have had the resources to indulge themselves in this way.

Young Imperial Army officers pose outside their barracks wearing double-breasted dark blue woollen overcoats with black fleece collars and gilt buttons. Their field caps bear the Imperial badge in gold, and their rank of second-lieutenant is indicated by a single gold stripe around the cap band (apparently partly marked here by the patent-leather chinstrap) and the cuffs.

lieutenant and captain; 2 buttons and 1–3 bands, major, lieutenant-colonel and colonel; and 3 buttons and 1–3 bands, brigadier-general, general and army commander.

The rank system used by the New Army was complicated and changed several times between 1904 and 1911. From 1904 ranks were shown on the cap band and on the cuffs of the soldier's tunic, lower ranks using a system of 1–3 braid bands around both. The officers' field cap also bore 1–3 vertical braids at the sides of the crown; the sequence went from 1 braid around the band and 1 vertical braid for a 2nd lieutenant, to 3 braids around the band and 3 vertical braids for a general officer.

In 1911 a new collar-patch rank system was introduced that was certainly used by at least some troops before the fall of the Qing Dynasty. The NCO grades from corporal up to colour-sergeant used 1–3 six-point yellow stars and a bar, set on a collar patch in the arm-of-service colour (red for infantry, yellow for artillery, white for cavalry, blue for engineers, and black for transport troops), below black Arabic numbers identifying the unit. (This system was continued into the Republican period only slightly modified, but the ranking was transferred from the collar to the shoulder straps of the tunic.)

Flags, 1840–1911

Flags were a dominant feature of all Chinese armies up until 1911, and were carried into battle in what seemed to Western eyes to be ridiculously high numbers. At one time every other soldier carried a standard or flag of some kind, and even in the 1890s one 300-strong unit had no fewer than 40 flags.

This Vickers machine-gun crew of a New Army division are seen taking part in one of the annual grand manoeuvres that took place almost every year from 1900 to 1910. All the soldiers wear the 1908 dark blue winter uniform, with branch-colour shoulder straps and cap bands, and here with manoeuvre brassards around the left arm. Note (foreground) the different numbers of yellow rank stripes around the cap bands and cuffs. Uniforms worn by the officers of the newly modernized Imperial Army varied widely; in this case the officer (left) wears light khaki summer uniform with black rank stripes around his forearms, but appears to wear the blue winter cap. His riding boots are black, but much non-regulation officers' field equipment in brown leather was bought from Japanese sources.

During the 19th century the Eight Banners of Manchu troops all carried flags with a dragon design in the centre of the field. The Banner colours were: 1st, yellow; 2nd, white; 3rd, red; 4th, blue; 5th, yellow with red border; 6th, white with red border; 7th, red with white border; and 8th, blue with red border. At the lower unit level, each battalion had a distinctive flag and a commander's flag, which might be triangular or square. Each company had two flags which followed the same pattern as the battalion flags, but in different colours. The colour of the company flags indicated the unit's position within the larger formation, as follows: red = vanguard; blue = left flank; white = right flank; yellow = centre; and black = rearguard. As part of the rearguard of a formation the artillery used black flags, often with a white border.

Green Standard flags usually had that colour of field, with a red border that was normally scalloped or serrated along the edges. Yung-Ying units do not appear to have had a rigid flag system, but as they were recruited locally and bore personal loyalty to their founder/commander they often featured his name in Chinese characters in the centre. Other flags seen in service had a red field with a yellow border and the formation's name across the centre in white characters. Another example was triangular with a red field, yellow scalloped border, and four white discs running across the centre, each disc with a different black character making up the commander's name or unit title.

Above most flags up to three horsehair tufts were attached to the pole, usually red but sometimes black. A smaller pennant or a group of coloured streamers was also often flown above the main flag. The streamers could come in any colour but were often in yellow, blue, red,

white and/or black; period illustrations appear to show that pennants were also barred in the same colours, up to a total of five. These five colours were adopted for the flag of the Chinese Republic after 1911, and were used until 1928.

Flags carried by the New Army from 1903 until 1911 usually had a plain red field with commanders' names, unit and army names in white characters. This type of flag continued in use during the Republican period until the victory of the National Revolutionary Army in 1928.

Imperial Army soldiers in action during the 1911 Revolution. These men belong to one of the better-equipped divisions, and wear the latest light khaki uniforms with the newly introduced 1911 collar patches; note (left foreground) a patch with a black three-digit Arabic unit number above a gold bar and rank stars. One thing all these men lack is a regulation Imperial cap badge, either the large dragon type or the small round cockade; its absence might suggest that they have switched sides to fight for the Revolutionaries.

A young military officer poses in his 'off-duty' clothing in Yunnan province in 1900. He may be on a tour of the region under his control, as he has two of his unit's standard-bearers with him. His bodyguard wear long baggy shorts with their long-sleeved tunics, which have coloured borders and bear identification characters. They are unarmed apart from traditional swords, which were often carried by Yunnanese troops before 1911.

PLATE COMMENTARIES

A: IMPERIAL ARMY 1840s–60s

A1: Cavalry bowman, Army of the Eight Banners, 1840–41

This bowman is a Manchu Bannerman, his elite status within the Imperial Army hierarcky symbolized by his choice of weapon. The bow was the weapon of choice among the Manchus, who were supposed to spend many hours practising archery. The red top of his Manchu hat rises to a 'pearl', and two squirrel tails hang down at the back. The long tunics came in a variety of colours, often (but not in this case) the colour of the Banner or corps to which the soldier belonged. The wealth of the bowman would be shown by the quality of his bow and equipment, and this archer has gold decoration on his belt; note too the bowcase hanging behind his hip. Most bowmen are seen with no other arms, relying on protection from the spearmen and other soldiers in their unit. Mounted archers carried up to 50 arrows in quivers slung on the back, and 30 was the minimum carried when going on campaign; while practising on foot this archer has stuck a sheaf of arrows in his belt for quick access.

A2: Halberdier, Tseng Kuo-fan's Army, 1856

Tseng Kuo-fan was one of the leading Imperial generals in the 15-year war against the Taiping Rebellion. This soldier wears the blue turban which was in common use throughout the 19th century. Over his white smock he wears a sleeveless jerkin with a yellow linen patch at front and back, bearing the Chinese character for his general's family name 'Tseng'. His blue trousers are worn with off-white leggings and cloth slipper-type shoes. He must be one of the slightly wealthier foot soldiers of Tseng's command, since he has purchased himself a fighting sword, but his billhook-style weapon has been simply made in a local smithy and lacks the decoration sometime seen on such weapons.

A3: Matchlock man, Mongolian Left Banner, 1860

This soldier, again distinguished by his Manchu hat, belongs to the Banner Army of the Mongolian general Sengge Rinchen, whose troops fought successfully against the British and French in 1860. His long red cotton tunic bears an identification patch, divided on the chest by the front opening, bearing the name of his commander and the Banner he serves in. His loose-legged trousers are just visible gathered at the ankles under his tunic; note the white stockings and thick-soled shoes. The usefulness of the matchlock, which remained popular in Chinese armies surprisingly late, was naturally limited by its short range and vulnerability to rain. Eyewitnesses mentioned the danger of a wounded man's smouldering match-cord setting light to his flammable clothing, and the bamboo powder-charge cartridges carried around the waist could also be hazardous to the soldier and his comrades.

B: STANDARD-BEARERS, 1850s–80s

B1: Corporal, Ever Victorious Army, 1864

This flag-bearer of the European-officered Ever Victorious Army, fighting against the Taiping rebels, is wearing its standard winter uniform, and apart from its green turban and Chinese shoes he might belong to many Western armies of the 1860s. His dark blue woollen jacket with red facings in fact has small white Chinese characters along the red shoulder straps, but his rank is shown by white chevrons on both sleeves, and his sidearm is a Beaumont Adams revolver. As

far as is known the EVA did not carry the numerous flags displayed by other Imperial Army units; the banner illustrated is always described as that of the Ever Victorious Army, and may have been the only design carried.

B2: Tiger man, Yeh Ming'ch'en's Army; Canton, 1857

This soldier of Yeh Ming'ch'en's Imperial force is part of the garrison defending Canton from British attack in 1857. Tiger men were an exotic 'shock force' of the 19th-century Imperial Army, and were often seen in complete striped costumes. On this occasion the standard-bearer has only donned the Tiger headdress with his standard uniform, a short blue tunic and yellow trousers covered with blue leggings; the chest disc bears the family name of his general, 'Yeh'. The traditional winged-tiger flag (here with coloured streamers) was probably not particular to the Tiger units, but one like this was captured at Canton; the tiger and other decorations on the flag are made from gold foil. The Tiger man's stripy cloth headdress had a bamboo inner structure which was supposed to provide some protection; like his bamboo shield decorated with a tiger's mask design, it was naturally useless against firearms.

Two young soldiers pictured in the late 1890s show variation in clothing worn even within a platoon. Their large blue turbans are the same, and were probably issue items; their tunics are identical, with the characters for 'front rank' and 'Chun Army' on the chests. Their trousers are not standard issue, however, and the soldiers may well have purchased them from a market or even brought them from home. Although their weapons are not easily identifiable they may be elderly US Springfield M1861 rifle-muskets, which were sold to China in large numbers.

Nearly all Chinese troops at this time were armed with spears, halberds, bows, or straight swords such as the one carried by this man.

B3: Standard-bearer, Kwangtung Victorious Army, 1885

This 'brave' belongs to the non-regular militia raised by the general Chang Chih-tung to fight alongside other Yung-Ying or 'Brave Armies' in 1885, and he immediately recruited German instructors to train it. Typically, the flag bears the character for his family name, with a small red tuft and small striped flag at the top of the pole. In contrast, the cloth disc worn on the chest of his highly decorated jacket displays the single character for 'Yung' or 'brave'. These regional battalions were established largely outside the regular Qing military structure, and usually proved superior to the Banner and Green Standard units.

B4 & B5: *Yung-Ying* standards, late 19th century

These unidentified scalloped flags are taken from drawings by European eyewitnesses, and probably identified Yung units or formations. A wide variety of flags were carried by the Imperial forces, and their sizes and designs often depended on the whim of commanders. The red flag **B4** has a commander's name on the yellow central disc, and a yellow horsehair tuft is just visible at the top hoist corner. **B5** has a commander's name in red on the black square, and good-luck symbols in yellow around the edges of the red field. It too has a hair tuft on the pole, below a small pennant whose colour probably identified a unit within a formation. We show both standard-bearers in typical period uniforms, and **B5** has a simple white fabric backpack as described by eyewitnesses.

C: CHINESE BORDER TROOPS, 1870s–80s
C1: Tso Tsung-t'ang's Army, Kansu province, 1872

This 'brave' of the general Tso Tsung-t'ang's army is fighting against Moslem rebels in a winter campaign during the first Dungan Rebellion. He is wearing winter clothing typical of the northern Chinese borders, with a fur hat and wadded cotton jacket. This loose garment, worn over several other layers of clothing (probably including his everyday uniform), displays the Chinese character for 'Tso'. The trousers are also of wadded cotton, and are worn with the warm, comfortable Mongol-type boots in common use with the Imperial Army. He is typical of his period in having minimal equipment, with only a canvas bag slung behind him to carry personal gear. His Dreyse M1841/48 rifle is a fairly modern type for the Imperial Army to have in service at this time, and proved superior to the firearms used by Russian militia during Siberian/Manchurian border clashes.

C2: Yunnan auxiliary, Tang Ching-sung's Army; Tonkin, 1884

The civilian clothing of this locally recruited volunteer from Yunnan province has been militarized in the most basic way, by the addition of identification discs with the Chinese character for 'Tang'. General Tang's men were sent by the Imperial government to fight alongside the Chinese-armed Black Flag mercenaries against the French in North Vietnam. His bamboo sun hat may have been issued, but is just as likely to have been bought in a local market. Although poorly dressed he is well armed; 2,000 Remington 'rolling block' breech-loading rifles had been bought to supply troops fighting against the French, and he has also acquired a captured LeMat revolver.

C3: Black Flag standard-bearer; Tonkin, 1884

The Black Flags and their Yellow Flag rivals were Chinese irregulars, largely refugees from the Taiping armies defeated by the Qing Dynasty in the 1860s, who had settled as bandits in the highlands of North Vietnam. Although still generally hostile to the regime they were happy to fight against the invading French when incited to do so by local mandarins in 1883–84, and the Chinese were willing to arm them as proxies rather than sending more Imperial troops into Vietnam. This mercenary carries a flag of the colour that gave them their name, bearing the white Chinese character for 'command'. The white cloth disc on his jerkin displays the black character for 'Liu', for the Black Flags' formidable leader Liu Yung-fu. He is wearing a large sun hat as used by many troops in southern China, and is armed with an Enfield P1853 muzzle-loading percussion rifle-musket. Local machetes were also commonly carried; the Black Flags routinely took heads, for which mandarins paid a scale of bounties (the highest being for a European officer). The Black Flags usually wore bandoliers, but witnesses also report some wearing sleeveless vests looped for cartridges.

D: THE SINO-JAPANESE WAR, 1894–95
D1: Rifleman, Huai Army, 1894

This soldier from an elite Imperial force raised by Li Hung-chang is wearing the distinctive Manchu hat with red crown; note too his hair dressed in the long traditional pigtail hanging down the back. His decorative double-breasted silk tunic fastens with ties down the right side; it is in the common colours of blue and red, with yellow and white piping. On his chest the white linen disc carries the soldier's number, unit number and other information. Loose-fitting silk breeches are worn tucked into black Mongol boots. Both equipment and weaponry used by this soldier are some of the best available to the Imperial Army in 1894–95. The German black leather belt with a white-metal buckle and box-like cartridge pouches was probably delivered along with the Mauser M1871 rifle. Modern rifles like this were used in some units alongside bows, swords and spears.

D2: Irregular cavalryman, Northern Border Army, 1895

The troops defending the borders of the far-flung Qing Empire were often poorly clothed, armed and trained. This cavalryman from the northern provinces has been sent to join the fight against the Imperial Japanese Army wearing a practical if non-standard dress of a fur-lined green winter jacket over a long Mongol-type *kaftan* coat. Hats lined with sheep- or yak-skin came in a wide variety of styles. As far as can be discovered, these irregulars tended not to wear insignia. Many were pictured with muskets and swords in 1895, but the lance was a favourite weapon of the northern and north-western horsemen. This rider's sword may well be a prized family heirloom passed down over generations. The French P185[ ] 'Minié' percussion-lock rifle worn over his shoulder is a leftover from the wars of the mid-century; ammunition would have been in short supply, particularly to irregular troops during the chaos of the Sino-Japanese War.

D3: Spearman, Ma Yu-kun's Army; Korea, September 1894

General Ma's was one of four formations of the 15,000-strong Imperial force at the battle of Pyongyang on 15 September. Although many Imperial soldiers were by now armed with rifles, others had to make do with more archaic weaponry; th[ ]

Troops from Kiangsu province march through the streets of Shanghai in the late 1890s, wearing straw 'boaters' and brightly coloured uniforms. Although silk jackets were worn as battle dress, it seems improbable that the coloured panels hanging from the waistband were worn in the field. All these men carry Berdan II rifles – a single-shot, bolt-action, .42cal (10.7mm) US design adopted in 1870 by the Imperial Russian Army. These may have been imported into China from the original manufacturer, Birmingham Small Arms in England, or bought from the Russian factories that produced them from 1875.

unfortunate man faces Japanese bullets armed with a spear and protected only by a bamboo shield. His black-bordered red uniform jacket shows a white cloth disc with Chinese characters identifying him as a front-rank man under the command of Ma Yu-kun. Many of the shields also bore such information, or were decorated with the face of an animal or a mythical beast, but in this case it has been left plain. Note his bare legs and straw sandals.

E: SINO-JAPANESE WAR & FORMOSAN REPUBLIC, 1895–96

E1: Li Hung-chang, 1896
Li Hung-chang was one of the most prominent Chinese political and military figures of the late 19th century. During the 1860s he raised substantial forces to successfully crush the Taiping Rebellion; in later decades he rose to become a wise counsellor to the headstrong Dowager Empress, and a statesman who earned the respect of foreign diplomats. His yellow silk jacket was an honour awarded to Li for his long service to the Dynasty, and on his left breast he wears the gold insignia of the Order of the Double Dragon 1st Class; the British sash and enamelled cross are those of a Knight Grand

Cross of the Royal Victorian Order, which was awarded to Li on his visit to London in 1896. Hardly visible here, another sign of his illustrious rank is the peacock feather hanging behind his Manchu hat.

E2: Captain, Imperial Army; Weihaiwei, 1895
This shows a typical uniform worn by junior officers during the Sino-Japanese War. The dark blue turban was more practical than the Manchu hat. His black silk jacket has blue and yellow silk decorative panels, though these might also be in a velvet material. Ranks were usually shown on this type of tunic by gold or yellow bands above the cuff, and subalterns and captains wore one to three bands. His winter trousers of blue wadded cotton are tucked into the very common soft Mongol boots. Hanging from his belt is an Imperial cavalry sabre, most of which were imported from Japan. The revolver tucked into his belt is a 12mm Lefaucheux M1858, one of several French handguns imported by the Chinese to arm their officers.

E3: Standard-bearer, Army of Ch'iu Feng-chia; Formosa, 1895
Formosa was ceded to the Japanese under the terms of the peace treaty forced on the Imperial government at the end of the Sino-Japanese War, but local politicians, with the support

This Formosan tribal fighter was photographed in the late 19th century, and may well have fought for the island's short-lived republic in 1895. The garrison that resisted the Japanese invasion was a mix of indigenous volunteers and Imperial regular and mercenary troops; it even included Liu Yung-fu, the old Black Flag general from Tonkin, with some of his men.

of the Qing garrison, refused to accept Japanese occupation. Among the 75,000 defenders of Formosa were 10,000 men under the command of Ch'iu Feng-chia, a Formosan patriot and poet. This soldier carrying the flag of the short-lived Republic of Formosa is a former member of the Qing garrison; he still wears his old uniform, but has covered the name of his former commander with a new chest patch showing Ch'iu's family name. The combined Qing and Formosan defenders were eventually defeated by a Japanese expeditionary corps sent to occupy the island; Ch'iu, like several other Formosan and Qing commanders, had deserted his men at the start of the fighting.

F: MODERNIZED ARMIES, 1900–08
F1: Cavalryman, Army of General Ma; Manchuria, 1904
This trooper of the Imperial cavalry serving in Manchuria at the time of the Russo-Japanese War, which spilled over into Chinese territory, wears a modernized type of uniform. His loose-fitting cotton peaked cap was made locally (clearly with more of an eye to practicality than smartness), and the khaki padded cotton tunic and trousers are a more serviceable

version of the late 19th-century Imperial Army uniform. This soldier belongs to the forces of a General Ma; at least four generals of that family name served the Dynasty in the north-west, starting with the Moslem leader Ma Zhan'ao who defected from the rebels to the government in 1872 during the first Dungan Rebellion. Whichever this one was, he must have had a relationship with the Japanese Imperial Army, since his trooper has an 11mm Murata Type 13 (1880) single-shot, bolt-action rifle and Japanese leather equipment. He also carries slung on his back a large traditional *da-dao* fighting sword, as used by some cavalry units in northern China and Manchuria.

F2: Rifleman, Mei Tung-yu's Army; Tientsin, 1902
This soldier is from one of the often small modernized commands that were springing up all over northern and central China during the period 1895–1905. Straw 'boaters' had already been worn by a few Chinese armies, and by the late 1890s they were widely seen; the characters on the band of this example presumably give information about the soldier and his unit. His tunic is typical of even modernized units, which continued to wear colourful clothing; again, the decorative panels might be in the same silk or in a contrasting material. This whole unit seem to have worn Mongol boots. Equipment is limited to a brown leather belt supporting what appears to be a single French M1869 ammunition 'pocket', for the French-supplied 11mm Chassepot M1866 single-shot, bolt-action rifle.

F3: Rifleman, Vanguard of the Right Division; Shantung province, 1903
This soldier is part of a large force raised by the general Yuan Shi-kai in Shantung in 1900 to protect the long coastline of the province. Yuan was always looking for any excuse to expand his army, and later in the same year he recruited four new battalions and converted provincial troops into regulars. This man wears the older style of uniform with a black turban, dark blue wadded cotton jacket and black wadded trousers and Mongol boots, as worn by large numbers of Imperial troops until the 1911 Revolution. Just visible on his chest are the two black Chinese characters for 'bodyguard', showing that he belongs to an elite unit within the division. His equipment is an Austro-Hungarian belt and pouches carrying 5-round *en bloc* clips for his 11mm Mannlicher M1886 bolt-action rifle.

G: IMPERIAL ARMY, 1908–11
G1: General, parade uniform, 1908
Introduced in 1900, the uniform worn by this *shang-chang* was still seen in use up to 1911. Apart from the Manchu hat, which was then being replaced by Western-style peaked caps, and the wide cuffs of the jacket, the uniform is largely Westernized. The hat crown has a red stone 'pearl' at the apex to signify his senior mandarin grade (junior grades wore a white 'pearl', and intermediate grades blue). The dark blue tunic with gilt buttons shows a mixture of insignia styles: the cuff bands of the 1890s are retained below new Austrian-style sleeve-knots in triple braid; the shoulder boards, with three gold buttons on interwoven gold cords on red backing, are of the German type, as are the red *Lampassen* stripes and piping on the black riding breeches. The standing collar is edged and piped gold and bears a badge of a gold dragon with a red pearl in its mouth. A dragon also appears on the gilt buckle-plate of the patent leather sabre belt; the gold sword-knot varied slightly in design to distinguish the three general-officer ranks.

G2: Cavalryman, Imperial Guard, 1910

This trooper of the Imperial Guard Division is wearing the cap and tunic of the uniform that was designed for the Emperor's elite unit, but photographs suggest that in practice many Guardsmen were still issued with standard light khaki or dark blue service uniforms. This trooper's light grey peaked cap has red crown piping and a band in the cavalry's white arm-of-service colour, with the round cockade badge introduced by the 1904 dress regulations and worn thereafter by some Imperial troops below officer rank. The new light grey cotton tunic, unusual in having breast pockets, has cavalry-white shoulder straps bearing a red Arabic '1' for the 1st Imperial Division. His khaki cavalry breeches and brown boots are standard Imperial Army issue; his sabre is of a model introduced in the late 19th century and usually manufactured in Japan. His carbine is the fully-stocked German 11mm single-shot, bolt-action Mauser M1871, the standard cavalry type imported in large numbers.

G3: Infantry private, Tibet, 1910

This *i-teng ping* of the expeditionary force that invaded Tibet in 1910 is wearing an improvised field uniform for winter campaigning. His standard dark blue peaked cap, with a red infantry band and the cockade badge, has had a fur ear-and-neck flap added to protect him against the bitter weather. The padded blue cotton jacket and trousers were specially issued during the 1910 campaign, and he has added the red infantry shoulder straps removed from his dark blue winter service uniform worn beneath it. By now leather ankle boots were regulation, but the old Mongol boots were much more practical in extreme cold. His weapon is the 7.92mm Mauser Gewehr 88 rifle – one of the latest bolt-action repeaters then being imported – firing smokeless ammunition. He appears to have only one German M1874/87 or M1895 cartridge pouch on his belt, together with the frogged bayonet scabbard.

H: THE 1911 REVOLUTION

H1: Colour-sergeant of infantry, New Army

This *shang-shih* wears the light khaki summer version of the 1904 regulation uniform, with the addition of the new collar insignia introduced in 1911. His unit/rank insignia are worn on a collar patch in the infantry's red arm-of-service colour; this bears a black Arabic '2' identifying his regiment, above a narrow gold bar and three gold stars. Hidden here by his two wide canvas ammunition-clip bandoliers are red tunic shoulder straps, with appliqué white Chinese characters giving unit and other details. On his belt are two German box-type ammunition pouches, and he carries the Mauser Gewehr 88 rifle.

H2: Volunteer, Revolutionary Army

Many Revolutionary troops in 1911 wore Imperial Army uniforms with insignia removed, civilian clothing, or black student uniforms; this young volunteer is wearing an Imperial Army winter uniform stripped of its insignia, and is distinguished by a white armband round the left sleeve worn as a Revolutionary field sign. Unlike most Imperial tunics this man's jacket has flapped breast pockets. From photographic evidence it appears that many Revolutionary troops 'roughed up' their Army caps by removing the stiffening. His leather belt equipment is again ex-Army issue, as is his Winchester rifle (presumably a .45cal M1876), and he also carries a small canvas haversack.

H3: Standard-bearer, Revolutionary Army

This rebel retains his uniform from previous Imperial service as a Green Standard soldier: a dark blue turban, and lighter blue winter jacket and trousers of wadded cotton. Although many

Yuan Shi-kai (1859–1916) was the dominant Chinese military commander for more than 20 years. His command of the forces protecting the Imperial family during the Boxer Rebellion in 1900 enhanced his position at the Qing court, and after playing only a minor part in the Sino-Japanese War he was appointed commander of the First New Army in 1895. The control over the Imperial military exercised by New Army officers under Yuan's influence was resented by other factions, leading to his forced retirement in 1909, but two years later he was summoned back, and was responsible for negotiating the largely peaceful abdication of the Qing Dynasty. As the strongman of the new Republic he almost immediately displaced Sun Yat-sen as president in February 1912; he died in 1916 shortly after having tried to found a new Imperial dynasty with himself as emperor. Compare the uniform he wears here with Plate G1.

Green Standard troops remained loyal to the Dynasty, others, who had not been paid for months, happily joined the Revolutionary Army. Over his shoulder he wears a sash with a slogan extolling the fight to overthrow the Qing Dynasty, and note again the white brassard. He has been given the honour of carrying one of the new flags based on the standard raised over the revolutionary headquarters in Wuchang. At each point of the black eight-point star is a yellow disc, with a further eight in a circle around the centre of the star. Given the burden of the standard (and since rifles were anyway in short supply), he has been issued with an ancient English-made Colt Navy 'cap and ball' revolver, which he has tucked into a waist bandolier.

INDEX